IT'S TIME TO EAT DEEP-FRIED MAC & CHEESE

It's Time to Eat DEEP-FRIED MAC & CHEESE

Walter the Educator

Silent King Books
A WhichHead Entertainment Imprint

Copyright © 2024 by Walter the Educator

All rights reserved. No part of this book may be reproduced in any manner whatsoever without written per- mission except in the case of brief quotations embodied in critical articles and reviews.

First Printing, 2024

Disclaimer

This book is a literary work; the story is not about specific persons, locations, situations, and/or circumstances unless mentioned in a historical context. Any resemblance to real persons, locations, situations, and/or circumstances is coincidental. This book is for entertainment and informational purposes only. The author and publisher offer this information without warranties expressed or implied. No matter the grounds, neither the author nor the publisher will be accountable for any losses, injuries, or other damages caused by the reader's use of this book. The use of this book acknowledges an understanding and acceptance of this disclaimer.

It's Time to Eat DEEP-FRIED MAC & CHEESE is a collectible early learning book by Walter the Educator suitable for all ages belonging to Walter the Educator's Time to Eat Book Series. Collect more books at WaltertheEducator.com

USE THE EXTRA SPACE TO TAKE NOTES AND DOCUMENT YOUR MEMORIES

DEEP-FRIED MAC & CHEESE

It's snack time now, hooray, hooray!

It's Time to Eat
Deep-Fried Mac & Cheese

A golden treat is on its way.

Crunchy, crispy, soft inside,

Deep-fried mac and cheese, oh, what a ride!

Little bites, all round and neat,

Mac and cheese becomes a treat.

Cheesy noodles, so warm and gooey,

Inside a crust that's crisp and chewy.

Dip them in ketchup or something new,

Barbecue sauce or ranch will do.

One big bite, oh, what a taste!

Deep-fried fun, no time to waste!

Hot from the pan, so nice and warm,

A snack that's perfect in any form.

Round like a ball or square like a block,

They're crunchy surprises, tick-tock, tick-tock!

It's Time to Eat
Deep-Fried Mac & Cheese

The cheese inside, it melts so quick,

Stretchy and stringy, just take your pick.

The noodles hug the cheese so tight,

Deep-fried mac and cheese is a delight!

Little hands reach out to share,

The cheesy goodness is everywhere!

We munch, we crunch, we're all so pleased,

With every bite of mac and cheese.

What's your favorite, crunchy or soft?

This snack has both, just lift it aloft!

Cheese lovers cheer, it's their dream come true,

Deep-fried mac is just for you!

Sharing is fun, so pass it around,

We all laugh with a joyful sound.

A snack so tasty, a moment so sweet,

It's Time to Eat
Deep-Fried Mac & Cheese

Deep-fried mac and cheese can't be beat!

The plate is empty, oh no, it's gone!

But don't be sad, we'll make more anon.

Cheese and noodles, a perfect pair,

Deep-fried fun is always there!

So when it's snack time, let's all say,

Deep-fried mac will save the day!

Crunch and cheese, the perfect mix,

It's Time to Eat Deep-Fried Mac & Cheese

This tasty treat is our top pick!

ABOUT THE CREATOR

Walter the Educator is one of the pseudonyms for Walter Anderson. Formally educated in Chemistry, Business, and Education, he is an educator, an author, a diverse entrepreneur, and he is the son of a disabled war veteran. "Walter the Educator" shares his time between educating and creating. He holds interests and owns several creative projects that entertain, enlighten, enhance, and educate, hoping to inspire and motivate you. Follow, find new works, and stay up to date with Walter the Educator™

at WaltertheEducator.com

www.ingramcontent.com/pod-product-compliance
Lightning Source LLC
LaVergne TN
LVHW052011060526
838201LV00059B/3981